The Little
Book of
Inner Peace

For Mary

The Little
Book of
Inner Peace

Simple practices for
less angst, more calm

Ashley Davis Bush

An Hachette UK Company
www.hachette.co.uk

First published in Great Britain in 2017 by Gaia,
a division of Octopus Publishing Group Ltd
Carmelite House, 50 Victoria Embankment,
London EC4Y 0DZ
www.octopusbooks.co.uk
www.octopusbooksusa.com

Distributed in the US by Hachette Book Group,
1290 Avenue of the Americas, 4th and 5th Floors,
New York, NY 10020

Distributed in Canada by Canadian Manda Group,
664 Annette St., Toronto, Ontario, Canada M6S 2C8

ISBN 978-1-85675-367-8

A CIP catalogue record for this book is available
from the British Library.

Printed and bound in China

10 9 8 7 6 5 4 3 2 1

Commissioning Editor: Leanne Bryan
Editor: Pollyanna Poulter
Art Director: Juliette Norsworthy
Designer: Rosamund Saunders
Illustrator: Abigail Read
Senior Production Controller:
Allison Gonsalves

Contents

Introduction

What lies behind us
And what lies before us
Are tiny matters compared
To what lies within us.
Ralph Waldo Emerson

What is Inner Peace?

Ahhhh . . . Bliss. Serenity. Calm. Inner peace is a deep and abiding sense of contentment and tranquillity. You may have experienced such a feeling spontaneously, stimulated by a peaceful situation: a gorgeous sunset, a walk in the woods, resting in a bubble bath, watching flames dance in a fireplace.

But often those moments of peace seem to evaporate when the mind gets distracted or life becomes busy. The brilliant news is that true inner peace is not a fleeting condition, but rather a natural state of calm awareness that resides within us. We can learn to connect to this deep reservoir of peacefulness even in the face of difficult, stressful circumstances. The deepest serenity abides, come rain or shine, regardless of the conditions.

Imagine that you can experience inner peace, even as chaos rages around you:

- during a busy rush hour
- in the middle of a hospital emergency room
- during a high-stakes competition
- with children pestering you
- while visiting your in-laws.

At its fullest expression, deep inner peace is a response to life – a compassionate, rooted awareness – that is independent of external circumstances. Like the ocean depths, inner peace is expansive and stable. With practice, you can learn to quickly leave the choppy, wild waves at the surface and dive into the calm deep. You can learn to fill your days with the unflappable experience of peace.

If you're concerned that in order to achieve this exalted state of Zen-like serenity you'll have to wear robes, shave your head, meditate in a cave and adopt a Sanskrit name, let me put your fears at rest.

Anyone, anywhere, can live with a feeling of inner peace.

Inner peace is a way of being with life — a way that fosters curiosity, equanimity and acceptance.

However, dwelling in peacefulness doesn't mean that you're naïve or simple. Nor does it mean that you avoid, deny or minimize reality or life's many challenges. Living with inner peace means that you see both the difficult and the beautiful aspects of this world and view them from a calm vantage point.

How to Get There

If inner peace is always within reach, then how do you begin to access it? The solution is practice. This book offers an array of intentional, mindful pauses designed to quiet your mind, foster awareness and increase your connection to that rich reservoir of serenity. These simple peace practices will not only deepen your own sense of calm, but will also have a ripple effect on your work, your relationships and, ultimately, the world.

This little book is structured into seven sections: Grounded and Rooted, Relaxation, Equanimity, Acceptance, Gratitude, Compassion and Beyond Yourself. On each of these pathways to peace, you will find specific tools and strategies that harness the benefits of stillness, movement, mindfulness (the practice of being present in the moment), meditation, breathing, visualization, creativity and contemplation.

You may find that doing just one micro-practice will immediately calm you. But when you commit to transforming a practice into a regular habit, you will actually begin to rewire your brain. As the science of "neuroplasticity" has demonstrated, the brain has the ability to change in response to repetitive experiences. By using self-directed practices, you can strengthen the neural (nerve) pathways in your brain toward the experience and awareness of calm. Inner peace can actually become your new default setting.

So dive into this book and discover your own inner wellspring. Every day you have an opportunity to become aware of, and connected to, the inner peace that resides within you. Every day you can make the choice to dwell in tranquillity.

The Benefits of Inner Peace

People who regularly engage in peace practices:

- reduce their experience of anxiety, depression, anger and resentment
- are less reactive to events
- experience deeper degrees of contentment and calm
- show trust in the world
- have an awareness that peace is available in the present moment
- express more spontaneous gratitude
- experience life with more flow and less resistance
- behave more kindly toward themselves and others
- radiate a peaceful energy
- feel a broader connection to the world at large.

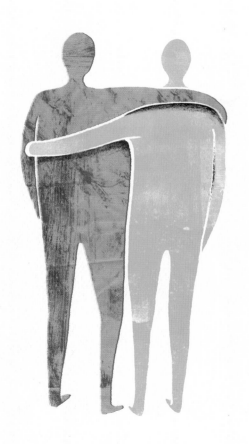

Peace . . .

It does not mean to be in a place where there is no noise, trouble or hard work. It means to be in the midst of those things and still be calm in your heart.

– *Anonymous*

1
Grounded and Rooted

We are living in a time in human history
when life seems to have become a cascade of tasks,
deadlines and constant accessibility to the dizzying
flow of news from around the globe. This non-stop
stream of stimulating information can be exciting . . .
and it can be exhausting.

The danger is that we become like tumbleweeds, tossed
and bounced in one direction and then another, in
response to the winds of circumstances that are beyond
our control.

The calmer alternative is to be deeply rooted and
stationary, even during the fiercest windstorm. When we
ground and root ourselves, we can withstand the stresses
of life with more ease, grace and stability.

A Circle of Love

We are relational beings, wired to attach to others on life's path. We are not meant to be isolated, shut off and withdrawn from our fellow sojourners. Human connection helps us to feel safe and sure. And the power of visualization allows us, at any time, to rekindle our connections and surround ourselves with people we have known and loved, from our past and our present.

Get in a comfortable position and close your eyes. Take a deep, low belly-breath. Imagine yourself in a beautiful open space, perhaps in a meadow or a spacious room. Make sure that your surroundings feel gentle, loving and serene.

In this comforting space, bring forward to surround you people and beings that you love.

- In your mind's eye, place in front of you people who supported you when you were young. You might include parents and grandparents, teachers, Scout leaders, church leaders or coaches. Whether these people are currently on the planet or not, envision them forming a semicircle in front of you. Imagine their love for you coming toward you in waves.
- Next, imagine friends who have mattered in your life – people who have supported you on the path of life for many years, or even those who may have walked only a short distance with you – and allow them to come into the circle.
- Now, imagine special beloved individuals and/or beings who love you. Have them start to close the circle behind you. These beings "have your back" and are emanating waves of love toward you. They could include your spouse, your children, your grandchildren, teachers, bosses, employees, mentors, in-laws, soul friends or other beings. Again, they may or may not be alive. Let them surround you and cast loving energy in your direction.

- Let all of these "benefactors" in your life come together and walk around you in this circle of love. You are encircled in their affection. Notice their smiles, the light from their eyes. Feel the warmth coming toward you, and feel warmth for them radiating out from within you.
- Rest in the calming, rooted sensation of being enveloped in so much rich love. Then open your eyes and proceed through your day, holding this love in your heart.

Grounded and Rooted

Talisman

A reporter once asked Barack Obama, President of the United States at the time, what was in his pocket. This is a favourite question amongst journalists, and is reported to have been asked originally of President Abraham Lincoln during the 19th century.

President Obama responded that he had a pocketful of charms – a rosary, given to him by the Pope; a tiny Buddha, given to him by a Buddhist monk; a lucky poker chip; and a small Coptic cross from Ethiopia. He is reported to have said that reaching into his pocket and touching the charms kept him grounded.

With the same intention, I often recommend to clients that they keep a small stone or trinket nearby. First, they select the object; and second, they imbue it with a trait. After that, they find that touching this talisman provides an immediate sense of comfort.

Try it for yourself.

- Select a special talisman – a stone, trinket or other small object – as a portable physical symbol. It might possess protective powers and/or symbolize a quality of peacefulness or strength. Or it might simply be a designated reminder to stop and centre yourself.
- Place it in a spot that is accessible to you. Consider your pocket, a purse or backpack or a desk drawer.
- Spend a moment each day holding your talisman in your hand. Let it be a literal touchstone to remind you of your strength, your passion, your purpose and your ever-present opportunity to pause intentionally and ground yourself. Let this simple object transport you to your centre, where inner peace truly resides.

Grounded and Rooted

Sensational

Although all we ever have is the present
moment, we so often live our lives preoccupied with
the past and the future. Being completely present in
the "now" has a way of waking us up.

Use the following sequence to help anchor yourself to the
present moment by tuning into your senses – especially if
you find yourself lost in worries, preoccupations or fears.
Begin by sitting in a comfortable place and selecting a
small object to hold.

- **See**: Notice the details of this object as you hold it.
  Pause and really *see* the nuances, the colours, the light
  reflected on it. Notice whether fine details sharpen
  into focus as you continue to gaze at the object.
- **Touch**: Feel the details of this object as you hold it.
  Rough. Smooth. Cold. Warm. Soft. Steely. Pause to
  investigate the textures, experiencing the sensations
  on your fingertips versus the palm of your hand.
- **Listen**: Now close your eyes and notice any sounds
  around you – distant, loud, quiet, repetitive, appealing,
  annoying. Listen to and label any sound that you hear:
  "snoring dog", "children laughing", "rain on roof",

"voices in the distance", "ambulance", "clock ticking", "wind blowing", "birdsong". Listen for the silence in and around the sounds.

- **Feel**: With your eyes still closed, draw your awareness inward. Scan your body to notice any areas of tension, tightness or tingling. Breathe space into each sensation. Notice places that normally don't get your attention: your elbow, your ankle, the back of your neck. Do your sensations change as you observe them?

We are sensual beings, with access to sensory experiences all day long. However, often we're so preoccupied that we miss most of what we're experiencing. Let your senses be the portal for awareness of this singular moment in time.

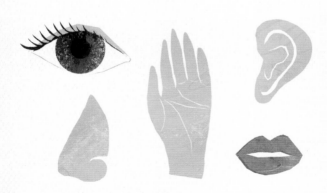

Grounding Breath

One of my teachers taught me this breathing technique as a tool for daily self-care. The professor suggested that this breath would keep me rooted, so that I could stay strong in the face of my clients' traumas, sorrows and struggles. I continue to use it during my workday even now, thirty years later.

This breath reaffirms your connection to the earth, to help ground you and sustain your energy.

- Stand strong or sit tall, with the soles of both feet on the floor.
- Imagine breathing through the soles of your feet, inhaling from the ground into your body.
- Feel warm, vibrant energy sourcing from the centre of the earth and coming up through your body.

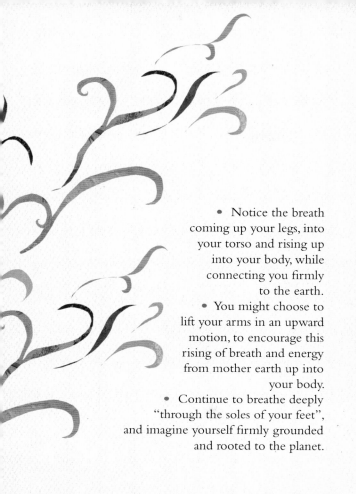

- Notice the breath coming up your legs, into your torso and rising up into your body, while connecting you firmly to the earth.
- You might choose to lift your arms in an upward motion, to encourage this rising of breath and energy from mother earth up into your body.
- Continue to breathe deeply "through the soles of your feet", and imagine yourself firmly grounded and rooted to the planet.

Grounded and Rooted

2
Relaxation

He who lives in harmony with himself lives in
harmony with the universe.
— *Marcus Aurelius*

Modern amenities (washing machines,
dishwashers, cars) have certainly "saved" us time,
compared to the lives of our ancestors. However,
we seem to have less leisure time than ever before.
Plus, we have even *more* things to do, with every
new technical advancement. Staying connected
requires a complex dance routine of monitoring
our emails, our texts, our Snapchats, our Facebook
and Twitter feeds . . . and so on and on. It may, at
times, feel impossible to unplug and relax.

In fact, because our brains are wired to enjoy and crave both novelty and connection, we get an addictive charge with each "data hit" from checking our devices for new information. Often, when we unplug, we can even feel a bit bored, because we're used to chronic stimulation.

Because productivity is highly valued, we stay on the treadmill of constant accessibility and productivity. We feel guilty when we disconnect for leisure time. We forget the need for replenishment and assume that "doing nothing" is slovenly and selfish.

Busy, stressed minds and bodies are roadblocks to inner peace. We require rest and relaxation in order to navigate our way to calm. When we find our way to pure, guilt-free relaxation, then inner peace lies just ahead.

Drumming

Drumming is one of the most basic elements of
music, in civilizations the world over. Rhythms unify
groups of people and are credited with healing and
expanding consciousness. From shamanic circles in
Indonesia, to a Beethoven symphony in Vienna, drums
add texture and a solid foundation to musical lines.

Drumming reduces stress, promotes relaxation, controls
pain, boosts the immune system and synchronizes the
two cerebral hemispheres of the brain. It brings us back
to the most essential element of life: our heartbeat.

The universe is saturated with vibrational energy.
According to quantum physics, everything from
the smallest subatomic particle to the largest star
has an inherent vibrational pattern. By participating
in drumming, we connect naturally with our own
vibrational state. And it can be surprising to discover
that the hypnotic trance of drumming is like a tonic
to the soul.

Use your hands or a pencil on a desk (you could even purchase a drum for your rhythmic musings). Drum for a minimum of 60 seconds. Pay attention to the timbre, rhythm, volume and tempo of your drumming:

- start slowly
- build in intensity of sound and volume
- finish slowly.

Notice how your body resonates with the beat and then relaxes after a short session of drumming.

Candle Contemplation

One of my favourite musical experiences is
singing "Oh Holy Night" on Christmas Eve, during
the candle-lighting section of the service. I stand
at the front of the church, facing the congregants
in almost complete darkness, and the organ begins
playing behind me.

"Oh Holy Night, the stars were brightly shining . . ."
One by one, candles are lit. A chain of candlelight on
the front row casts out the darkness. The large sanctuary
gradually fills with the warm glow of candlelight
reflecting off beaming faces.

"Fall on your knees, Oh, hear the angel voices . . ."
Each new point of light really does feel like an
angelic burst.

Candlelight is a way to dress up a table, to romance a date,
to turn a bath into a spa and to create festivity during
a holiday. A single candle flame is mesmerizing, a simple
portal to stillness.

- Light a candle and place it in front of you.
- With "soft eyes" (partially closed, eyes relaxed), gaze at the flame.
- Label what you see: "dancing flame", "golden light", "blue centre" . . .
- Observe the movement.
- If your mind wanders (and it will), bring your attention back to the flame.
- Make blowing out the candle part of your experience as well. Watch the smoke curl upward. Imagine the stress in your life drifting away with the smoke.

Balasana

In yoga, this popular relaxing posture is called the "child's pose".

This calming pose stretches your lower back, hips, thighs, knees and ankles. It also relaxes your neck and spine. Simultaneously it increases blood flow to your head and calms the mind.

- Start by kneeling on a carpeted floor or mat.
- Drop your bottom toward your heels.
- Lean forward, stretching your body down so that your stomach is resting on your thighs and your forehead is resting on the ground (if this is difficult for you, you can place a pillow between your bottom and ankles, or between your chest and thighs).
- Bring your arms round beside your body, so that your hands are touching your feet (an alternate pose is to stretch your arms out in front of you – experiment and see which position is most relaxing for you).
- Rest in this position, letting your body sink into itself. Breathe normally.
- If your mobility is limited, you can simulate this position while sitting on a chair. Place a pillow on your lap, lean forward and embrace your legs.

Allow yourself to rest into this position for several minutes, inviting a sensation of inner relaxation.

Calming Breath

It is quite natural to encounter specific situations that trigger anxiety. Some common circumstances include: going to the dentist, speaking in public, meeting your boss, undergoing a medical procedure or flying in an aeroplane.

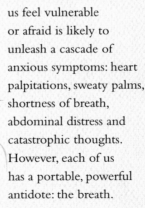

A situation that makes us feel vulnerable or afraid is likely to unleash a cascade of anxious symptoms: heart palpitations, sweaty palms, shortness of breath, abdominal distress and catastrophic thoughts. However, each of us has a portable, powerful antidote: the breath.

"Intentional breathing" is a deceptively simple, yet powerful ally for awakening feelings of inner peace. And, fortunately, your breath is ever-present.

This easy practice calms the mind, body and spirit. To prepare for it, find a comfortable sitting position.

- Relax your jaw.
- Bring your fingers to your lips and breathe in a deep, low belly-breath (touching your lips is known to activate the parasympathetic nervous system, your body's natural pause-button).
- Now place your hands in your lap, palms up, and breathe normally.
- On the in-breath, say or think these words: "Breathing in, I am calm."
- On the out-breath, say or think these words: "Breathing out, I am relaxed."
- Follow the sensations of your breath as it moves in and out of your body.
- Repeat this cycle for up to five minutes. Use a timer, so that you don't have to keep watching the clock.

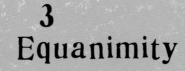

3
Equanimity

God, grant me the serenity to accept the
things I cannot change,
The courage to change the things I can,
And the wisdom to know the difference.
— *Reinhold Niebuhr*

The art of equanimity is found in our ability to maintain emotional composure and mental clarity, even during stressful times. It means staying anchored to our inner stability, so that we are not untethered by worry, anger, irritation or impatience.

This may sound too good to be true – as if it were a state of being only for awakened ones. However, equanimity can be cultivated through mindfulness. Begin by observing yourself: watch your reactions, take note of feelings as they manifest in your body, and watch thoughts as they arise in your mind.

Mindfulness is the practice of being present in the moment, and of observing our experience with tenderness. As we engage in mindfulness, over time we will become less reactive. The mindful practices in this section are signposts along the path to peacefulness within.

Serenity Syllables

When you use this technique, for those few moments it's like being on a spiritual retreat.

- Begin by closing your eyes and sitting down in a comfortable position.
- While you repeat the syllables SA, TA, NA and MA, touch the fingers of each hand to your thumb. It will look and sound like this (right hand and left hand):

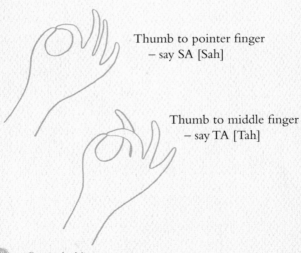

Thumb to pointer finger
– say SA [Sah]

Thumb to middle finger
– say TA [Tah]

Thumb to ring finger
— say NA [Nah]

Thumb to pinkie (little finger)
— say MA [Mah]

- Repeat this sequence using both hands simultaneously
  for six rounds:
  In the first two rounds, say the syllables out loud.
  In the second two rounds, whisper the syllables.
  And in the final two rounds, think the syllables silently
  in your head.
  You can deepen the calming effect by continuing the
  silent rounds for as long as you wish.

These Sanskrit syllables mean "birth", "life", "destruction"
and "regeneration". The tactile, patterned hand
movements help to promote focus, clarity and balance.

Wisdom Words

There once was a king who sought a phrase –
a mantra that could advise and guide him. He called
upon all the wise people in his land, asking them for
the perfect words that would be a compass for every
circumstance, in every place and time.

One of the wise men brought him a ring inscribed
with the phrase "This Too Shall Pass". The king kept the
ring and reflected upon the inscription when he was in
triumph, so that his ego was not too large. When he was
in trouble, he read and reflected on the words, so that his
heart was not too heavy. These words did, in fact, provide
a guiding light for him as he ruled the land.

This too shall pass

Both Eastern and Western traditions use a "mantra" – a
word or phrase – as the object of meditation or prayer,
and to offer a focal point, an anchor, for contemplation.

- Sit comfortably and close your eyes.
- Summon the words "This Too Shall Pass".

You may want
to imagine the
words written on
a vast expanse of
sky, or simply hear
them on your breath.

- When you become aware
  that your mind is drifting, return
  to repeating the words "This Too Shall Pass".
- After a few minutes, reflect on the meaning of the
  words and how the truth is manifest in your life.

Everything is changing all the time. The problems of
your present will eventually fade to the past. And the
joys you experience will change over time, too. Coming
to understand that "This too shall pass" helps you form
a foundation of equanimity.

Enjoy Your Non-Toothache

The wise Vietnamese spiritual teacher Thich Nhat Hanh talks about gaining inner peace via the path of noticing what you *don't* have. His classic example is to enjoy your "non-toothache". If you've ever had toothache, you will know it causes quite a bit of pain; in fact, when you have toothache, it's all you notice, all you can think about – you'd give virtually *anything* NOT to have toothache.

However, when the toothache is gone, you quickly forget about the pain and immediately begin to focus on other issues or concerns.

For this equanimity practice, write a list of ten things that, for today, you are currently NOT experiencing, but which would definitely be unpleasant if you were. In other words, write a list of "It could be worse" items. Here are a few of my personal favourites:

For today,

I enjoy *not* **being homeless**
I enjoy *not* **being in hospital**
I enjoy *not* **vomiting**
I enjoy *not* **having a migraine**
I enjoy *not* **declaring bankruptcy**
I enjoy *not* **going blind**
I enjoy *not* **being caught outside in a blizzard**
I enjoy *not* **losing my electricity**
I enjoy my car *not* **having a flat tyre**
I enjoy *not* **having a serious illness.**

So often we think about all the things we *do* have, but don't want (stress, deadlines, bills, and so on). It is a powerful practice to broaden our perspective by noticing all the things that we *don't* suffer from.

ABC Meditation

Sometimes people are daunted by the thought of meditation because it feels confusing or they believe they must dedicate 20–40 minutes to the process at a time. However, short meditations can be quite powerful. Even a few minutes of meditation can dramatically affect the trajectory of your day.

The components of this short practice are as simple as **ABC** – use the following as a guide, spending at least one minute on each section. Sit comfortably or lie down, and pay attention to the following:

A – Aware: First, notice your environment: any sounds around you, the temperature of the air on your skin, any smells, the texture of the chair or bed beneath you, how your body feels and whether there is any tension. Notice everything around you with a calm, non-judgemental curiosity. If you find your mind wandering (and you probably will), simply label it "thinking" and return to scanning your environment. This process anchors you in the present moment.

B – Breathe: Simply feel, listen to and watch the breath. Label your out-breath as "out-breath" and your in-breath as "in-breath" . . . "out-breath" . . . "in-breath" . . . and so on. If your mind wanders (and it will), label it "thinking" and then bring your attention back to the breath. Or imagine the thought as a cloud that just passes across the sky of your mind. Notice as the breath starts to draw your attention inward and prepares you for going to your centre.

C – Core: Begin by imagining a column of light that runs through the core of your body like a vertical axis, extending upward through the crown of your head and downward through your body. Let the light be a soothing colour and temperature. Allow yourself to merge into the centre and connect to this core column of light and energy.

4
Acceptance

If you let go a little, you will have a little peace. If
you let go a lot, you will have a lot of peace. If you
let go completely, you will have complete peace.
– *Ajahn Chan*

Acceptance is a direct route to inner peace.
People often misinterpret acceptance as apathy, a
lack of caring, nonchalance or avoidance. They think
that acceptance will lead to stagnation and paralysis.
"How can I accept poverty, injustice, domestic violence,
racial prejudice and other ills in the world?" "How can
I accept the parts of me that I need to change?"

But acceptance doesn't mean to condone or give up; rather it means to honour the reality of the present moment, even as we notice the possibility for change. When we struggle and fight against the current of life, we miss both the scenery and the opportunity to engage with the flow of the river.

A lot of our energy and happiness is lost, and stress created, by our everyday resistance to circumstances that are beyond our control: frustration with the weather, anger at traffic, sadness at other people's opinions, judgement of our ageing bodies. As we begin to change our relationship to the circumstances that surround us, from resistance to acceptance, we can experience feelings of new-found freedom and calm. Ironically, this is the very freedom that will help us skilfully change course and will empower us to create positive change.

Go with the Flow

I have heard a frequent refrain from many of
my clients through the years: *"I don't have time to
do anything for myself."* Of course, at some point we
have all felt as if we don't have time to . . . exercise,
meditate, read a book, go for a walk, visit a friend.
And many days it's true: we don't have time to fit in
a time-consuming, self-care practice.

However, there is something we always seem to find
the time to do every single day: wash our hands. What a
perfect opportunity to take a mindful pause. Furthermore,
the water itself is an ideal reminder of acceptance
qualities. Think of flowing rivers, waterfalls, rushing
currents, ocean waves . . .

- When you are at a sink washing your hands, take an
  intentional pause.
- Feel the temperature and pressure of the water as it
  cascades over your fingers.
- Breathe deeply and remind yourself to "let go" and
  flow *with* life, rather than against it.

- Think or say aloud the words, "I go with the flow of life" or "I align myself with the energy of now", or "I accept life as it flows in, around and through me" or "I am open to flow". Choose any acceptance words that resonate with you.

Tapping to Tranquillity

Tapping is a simple technique that combines the effectiveness of self-hypnosis, affirmations and acupressure. Originally called EFT (Emotional Freedom Technique), it is now generally referred to as "tapping". The aim is to tap on nine consecutive points while stating a simple phrase. Tapping can be used for almost any issue, but the following is a basic script to bring greater acceptance into your life.

Tapping is a very forgiving technique. You can use either hand for tapping on either side of your body, or tap on both sides of your body at the same time. Do whatever feels best for you.

First, rate yourself on a scale of 1 to 10, regarding how difficult/resistant you feel to a particular situation in your life: 1 = "easy to accept"; 10 = "very hard to accept".

Then use several fingers to tap gently on each point. The sequence consists of as many rounds as are required to bring your feelings of resistance down to a scale of 1.

Each round begins with an affirmation, while tapping on point 1:

- Tap on point 1 (the karate-chop point – the side of the hand between your pinkie/little finger and your wrist), saying out loud: "Even though it's hard for me to accept [state your situation], I deeply love and accept myself." Repeat these words two more times while tapping on the outside of your hand.

Continue the round by tapping several times on the following 8 tapping points, while saying the phrase once:

- Tap on point 2 (the inside of your eyebrow), saying out loud: "I feel so stuck."

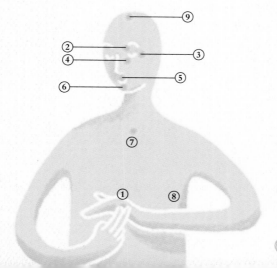

- Tap on point 3 (the outside of your eye), saying out loud: "I feel stuck in this situation."
- Tap on point 4 (underneath your eye, at the top of your cheek), saying out loud: "I am stuck."
- Tap on point 5 (underneath your nose, above your lip), saying out loud: "I feel stuck in this situation."
- Tap on point 6 (underneath your lip, above your chin), saying out loud: "I feel stuck in this situation."
- Tap on point 7 (on your sternum, between your collarbones), saying out loud: "I feel so resistant."
- Tap on point 8 (on the side of your body, underneath your arm), saying out loud: "I am tired of being stuck."
- Tap gently on point 9 (the top of the head), saying out loud: "I am open to something different."

Take a deep breath and rate yourself again on the same 1–10 scale. Notice if there has been any shift – a decrease in the scale's number. Keep tapping for several more rounds until the rating gets to 1, using the same words (or other words that resonate for you). The words are general guidelines, not absolutes. The main points are the tapping and your intention.

You can tap every single day to help clear resistance and promote acceptance in your life. Remember: acceptance of "what is" in the moment leads to inner peace.

Smile

We shall never know all the good
that a simple smile can do. Peace
begins with a smile.

— *Mother Teresa*

**Remember that inner peace is a state of
freedom** from external conditions. Resistance
to any aspect of the present moment creates
suffering. Acceptance, or allowing the present
moment to be as it already is, leads to peace.

The next time something occurs that causes some
inner resistance in you, some pressure
or negative reaction, just stop
and use a smile as an aid to
finding acceptance.

- Lift the corners of your mouth with your fingers – literally, putting a smile on your face. Let the smile remind you that acceptance is ultimately more powerful than resistance.
- Breathe deeply, then exhale slowly.
- Invite yourself to be curious about whatever set of circumstances has initiated your resistance.

Acceptance

Ask yourself:
"What might I learn from this situation?"
"Who do I want to be in this situation?"
"Where might these circumstances lead me?"
"What choices do I have?"

Smiling is known to affect moods positively. The act
of smiling activates neural messaging by stimulating
compounds called neuropeptides, and by regulating the
temperature of blood flow to the brain. And smiling
doesn't just improve your own mood – it's contagious.
It actually improves the mood of people around you.
So, in your attempt to bring greater acceptance into your
own life, smile and watch the ripple effect on the people
around you.

Recalibration Breath: 4-7-8

The 4-7-8 breath is an ancient breathing technique that restores and recalibrates the central nervous system. The combination of a short inhale followed by a twice-as-long exhale has an immediate effect on the parasympathetic nervous system (PSN). You can think of the PSN as the brakes on your stress response. When you practise the 4-7-8 restoration breath regularly, over time the effect is a calmer, less reactive disposition.

I have seen clients who are struggling with anxiety, anger and panic experience profound relief, simply by incorporating this practice into their routines, twice a day. Think of it as helping you drop your resistance, so that you can breathe into acceptance of "what is".

Acceptance

The breath:

- Inhale through your nose to the count of 4.
- Hold your breath to the count of 7.
- Exhale through your mouth, as if you are blowing air out through a straw, to the count of 8.
- Immediately repeat the cycle two more times.
- Do a three-cycle round in the morning and a three-cycle round in the evening.

This simple technique, saturates your bloodstream with oxygen and expels carbon dioxide from your lungs. The act of counting gives your mind a focal point as your body begins to relax.

5
Gratitude

I've suffered a great many catastrophes in my life.
Most of them never happened.
— *Mark Twain*

Gratitude is a fast track to happiness. Why? Because our mind becomes what it rests upon. If we allow our mind to rest upon all our troubles, all our stresses, all of the "weeds" in our life, then it will grow troubled and agitated. However, if we train our mind to notice our blessings, all of the "flowers" in our life, then it will become more satisfied and grateful.

The mind is like a torch, shining on either the sorrows or the joys, the problems or the solutions in our life. Fortunately, we hold the torch and get to choose where to shine it.

Gratitude is not just a state of being – it's a habit. And, like any habit, it requires training. When we train our mind to dwell in gratitude regularly, we will also dwell in peace.

Morning Thanks

The moment when you first wake up – before you even get out of bed – is a key time to shape your mood. You could think of all the things you have to do in the coming day . . . or you could think of all the things you get to do in the coming day. You have the power to set the tone: will the day be a burden or a blessing?

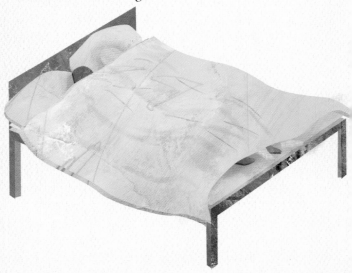

The Jewish practice of "Modeh Ani" is a morning prayer of thanksgiving for the gift of another day in which to live. This simple and beautiful ritual serves as the inspiration for this practice.

- Put a Post-it note or postcard beside your bed with the reminder, "I GIVE THANKS."
- While you are still in bed, put one hand on your upper chest and the other hand on your belly. This comfort-pose mimics the feeling of an infant being held to an adult's chest.
- Breathe into your hands and say the words, "I give thanks." Let the feeling of gratitude flood your body.
- Repeat for a minimum of three breaths.
- For added emphasis, include things for which you are grateful, such as "I give thanks that I'm alive and have another day to live", "I give thanks that I have a job I enjoy", "I give thanks that I have a family to love."

Intentionally saturate the beginning of your day with gratitude and watch how the day unfolds more smoothly.

Install the Positive

This technique, with the addition of soothing alternate tapping, is inspired by the practice of "Taking in the Good", as developed by the neuropsychologist Rick Hanson. Together, they work to imprint gratitude into your neural networks so that, over time, the temporary state of being thankful becomes a sustained trait of living in gratitude.

Before bedtime, sit down and take a moment to intentionally remember between one and three things that happened in your day and for which you are grateful. The following procedure helps you to re-experience the memory, and not simply list it.

- One at a time, bring to mind each event, occurrence or situation that you are recalling.
- Continuously tap right and left on your legs, as you summon details about the memory – colours, sounds, words, faces, feelings.
- Hold the memory in your mind and allow it to expand within you, filling your body with a sense of gratitude (keep tapping on your legs as you do this: right, left, right, left).
- Imagine that you are a sponge and are soaking up this feeling of gratitude, letting it saturate your body. Continue to tap gently.
- Hold this feeling for at least 20 seconds, filling yourself with the sensation of gratitude.

Instant Travel

An amazing truth is that your body and mind respond to what you imagine, even if it isn't real. For example, your body will relax, whether you literally lie in the sun on the beach or *visualize* yourself lying in the sun on the beach.

In fact you can use intentional visualization to shift your emotional state from one of anxiety to one of serenity and peacefulness. The aim is to imagine yourself in a beautiful place – somewhere that is comforting and pleasant, either real or fictional.

Try these suggestions to invoke instant holiday bliss. Close your eyes and imagine one of the following:

- A beautiful, beloved place that you have visited, either once or many times. It could be a once-in-a-lifetime holiday spot or a comforting, favourite place that you return to frequently.
- A happy time in your life that you wish to revisit. Perhaps your children are now grown-up and you want to think back to a time when they were small.

Perhaps you'd like
to recall a happy time
from your own childhood.
- A magical, fictional location: the perfect
mountain view, the ideal beach scene, the
secluded forest trail that opens to a waterfall.

Once you have your time and place, summon the
details in your mind's eye: temperature, sounds, smells,
sights and tastes.

Direct your attention to the positive feelings and
associations that arise in your body – warm
heart, relaxed feelings, a smile, and so on.
Breathe in deeply and let the feelings
of well-being expand within you.

Framing

Life has a way of speeding from one activity
to the next in a sort of "runaway train" feeling.
We wake up, rush to get children out of the door
and ourselves to our jobs, rush our way through
projects at work, rush our way to exercise, meals,
errands, homework, bath time, and then collapse
so that we can begin it all again the next day.

While life may feel like a seamless avalanche of
activities, there are actually many opportunities to
recognize transition points. One of the most obvious
places to recognize our transitions between activities is
at doorways – crossing thresholds. We can use each portal
as a place to pause, a vehicle for mindfulness. In doing so,
we allow the possibility of mindful appreciation.

The idea is to "frame" each experience as you transition
from "that – what you have just ended" to "this – what
you are just beginning". The intentional pause between
the two helps you stop and notice your life, right as you
are living it.

To do this, literally choose three doorways to help "frame" your transitions. I would suggest the door to your home, to your office and to your bedroom.

- As you leave a place, and before you transition to the next place (work, home), stop to touch the top or side of the door frame.
- Stop to think about what you just left, and what you were grateful for in that experience. Notice what you are about to enter, and what you are grateful for about the anticipated experience.
- You can take either seconds or minutes to complete this practice.

You don't want to wake up one day and wonder where your life went, almost as if you were so busy that you missed it. This slowing-down peace practice will help you savour your life, not just during special occasions, but every day, as you live it.

6
Compassion

One day a Native American grandfather was talking to his grandson. He said, "There are two wolves fighting inside all of us – the wolf of fear and hate, and the wolf of love and compassion."

The grandson listened, then looked up at his grandfather and asked, "Which one will win?"

The grandfather replied, "The one we feed."
– *Native American story*

Self-compassion is the art of being kind, loving, tender and accepting to oneself. It is an essential precursor to well-being and a vital skill in peaceful living. However, most people are incredibly hard on themselves, both in their thoughts (self-critical and judgemental) and in their behaviour (self-sabotaging and destructive). They find it difficult to be kind toward themselves. In fact, in our society we often confuse self-compassion with selfishness or weakness. Furthermore, we tend to prize stoicism and sacrifice over self-nurturing.

Yet, ironically, when we have self-compassion, we develop the ability to have compassion for others. When we really love ourselves and direct a tender kindness toward our own foibles, struggles and needs, we feel increasingly connected to other beings. Ultimately, when we step onto the pathway of self-compassion, we find that it radiates and reverberates, becoming a gateway to more compassion for others throughout the world.

Hand-Print Your Heart

Have you ever thought to yourself that you're an idiot, you're ugly, you're flawed, you're worthless? It's not uncommon to be plagued by such unflattering thoughts. Or perhaps you are unkind to yourself in other ways – by not eating well, by drinking too much, by skimping on exercise and sleep.

It is surprising how difficult it can be to be kind to ourselves, in both thought and deed. It's almost as if we can more easily become our own worst enemy than our own best friend. Self-compassion means being gentle and kind to yourself, even as you recognize your own frailties. An essential part of self-compassion is understanding that you share with every human on this earth the vulnerabilities of being flawed and mortal. This is all the more reason to be as kind to ourselves as we would be to others who suffer.

Use the following practice frequently, to develop a gentler, more accepting and loving attitude toward yourself.

- Place one or both hands upon your heart. This act alone stimulates oxytocin, a feel-good hormone.
- Shine tender light toward yourself. Feel a stream of light pouring into your head from above and filling your body with light.
- As your hand is on your heart, say to yourself one of the following:

"Even though I make mistakes, I accept myself."

"I deserve to be happy and I can love myself."

"I can learn to love myself, in spite of my flaws."

"May I be at peace. May I be happy."

"I am doing the best I can."

"Even though I sometimes feel inadequate, I am okay."

"I have an opportunity to grow every single new day."

- Take a deep breath.

Butterfly Hug

This technique helps to calm you if you are
feeling stressed or upset. It's also useful as a self-care
practice that develops a feeling of tenderness — a
core attribute of inner peace.

The "butterfly hug" was developed by Lucina Artigas,
who worked with survivors of Hurricane Pauline in
Acapulco, Mexico, in 1997. It uses the calming effect
of alternate tapping to calm the nervous system.

- Cross your arms over your chest, so that the tips of
  your middle fingers are below the collarbone.
- Interlock your thumbs to form the butterfly "body".
  Extend your fingers to make the "wings".
- Close your eyes or look softly down.
- For one to three minutes, alternate movement of
  your hands, so that the butterfly is flapping its wings
  (right hand taps your chest, left hand taps your chest).
  Try to keep your fingers pointing up toward the
  shoulders, and not sideways toward the arms.

- While tapping (or flapping the wings), breathe low and deep from the abdomen.
- Notice the sensations in your body.

Using this practice is a way to anchor self-comfort and self-soothing into your neural networks, which in turn leads to a regular feeling of peacefulness.

Wish Them Well

When you are waiting in a queue in a shop,
it is tempting to become frustrated. Often the
queue is moving slowly and you are in a hurry
to be elsewhere. Inner peace can easily go out of
the window.

I know . . . I lived in New York City for a decade and I
became quite accustomed to, and mostly impatient with,
long queues. I wish I had used this practice back then.

The next time you are waiting in a queue, stop and see
the opportunity before you. You have some time on your
hands with which to spread goodwill.

• View this moment as a chance to share and spread
  loving-kindness.
• Look at the person in front of you in the queue.
  Recognize that this person has known both joys and
  sorrows, dreams and disappointments. This person has a
  mother and a father, either alive or no longer alive. This
  person places his head on a pillow each night, hoping
  for a good night's sleep. This person may carry a world

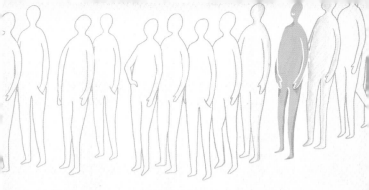

of burdens on her shoulders. Wish them well. Think to yourself: *I wish you peace. I wish you joy. I hope that you know happiness. I hope that you are free from suffering.* Mentally blow the well-wishes the person's way.

- Look at the person behind you in the queue and repeat the same process. Wish them well.
- When you get to the cashier, bank teller or assistant, once again, honour the shared human experience between you. You both know joys and sorrows. You both have dreams and disappointments. You both wish to be loved. Wish them well. Think: *I wish you peace. I wish you joy. May you know happiness. May you be free from harm.*

When you wish other people well, you dissolve your own sense of frustration, impatience and irritability. Create this loving-kindness within you and watch how you yourself benefit, even as you wish others well.

World Peace

When we access the deep peace within us,
we begin to radiate peacefulness out to the world.
The following is an energizing breathing practice,
designed to reinvigorate your body as it sets the
intention to spread peace
to others throughout
the world.

Fill your lungs with
three short, vigorous
inhales through your
nose, as if you are
sniffing. And as you do
this, think about those
who are suffering . . .

Compassion

- Sniff three times:
  Honouring those who live in physical and/or
  emotional pain.
  Then, breathe out a long exhale, sending loving
  kindness to these people.
- Repeat, sniff three times:
  Honouring those who live in fear.
  Breathe out a long exhale, sending compassion to
  these people.
- Repeat, sniff three times:
  Honouring those who are lonely.
  Breathe out a long exhale,
  sending well-wishes to
  these people.

It is natural to want to reduce
suffering and increase happiness.
Remember that we are all more
similar than we may imagine.

7
Beyond yourself

There are two ways to live:
you can live as if nothing is
a miracle; you can live as if
everything is a miracle.
—*Albert Einstein*

Gain Perspective

Take a good look at your stress levels and your list of worries. The chances are that your thoughts are mostly wrapped up with concerns about your own life – your finances, your workload, your relationships, your health. Of course this makes sense, since it is your life, after all.

However, a large part of accessing inner peace comes from our ability to step back and view our individual situation in a larger context, to cultivate perspective. Notice: there is a vast web of interconnected people of all ages, both near and far, who have their own struggles. There are entire natural systems that we might not be paying attention to – the world of insects, the animal kingdom, even a world underwater. And there are planets beyond our own planet, and galaxies beyond our own galaxy.

There is mystery in the universe, a kaleidoscope of patterns and designs that we do not fully understand. For many, this mystery points to a Divine source. Others speak of natural energy, or a natural law that science has yet to understand. Yet for all, there is mystery. We may connect with faith or science but, either way, there is something more, something beyond.

Giving ourselves the perspective of a much larger context can be a calming elixir. Whether we see the universe through a spiritual or naturalist lens (or both), knowing that we are a meaningful part of a larger system is a comforting truth.

Embrace Change

For several years I hosted a podcast called
"Embracing Change". What I loved about
planning each show was the ease with which
I could locate topics about change. *Everything*
could somehow be related to the idea of change.

I developed shows about ageing, the empty nest,
parenting, moving, new careers, marriage, divorce, as
well as about resilience and equanimity. Virtually any
life situation involves some kind of change.

My tag line was: "Remember – change is inevitable,
whether it happens to you or you make it happen.
Embracing change is a critical life-skill to help you live
with courage and choose peace." And so it is.

You can embrace or resist change, but it's still going
to happen. Use this practice to help you become
more friendly with change.

- Observe something in nature: a flower, a tree, a plant, even a piece of fruit. Notice that its current form is temporary. It was different weeks ago, and it will change in the weeks to come.
- Recall that all living things are impermanent and will pass away.
- Reflect on the fact that you, too, are impermanent and will pass away.
- Say the words, "I am learning to embrace change. I am trying to embrace change. I am open to embracing change."
- Breathe in the beauty of this moment – of NOW.

Cultivate Wonder

Sometimes we get so busy, so distracted,
so preoccupied and so stressed that we forget to
open our eyes and notice the world around us.
So, take an intentional pause and look, gaze and
cultivate wonder for the things around you, both
natural and man-made. Try looking from both of
these perspectives:

Macro-gazing: Look up and out.
* Start by looking up at the sky. Notice the colour of
  the sky, and whether or not there are clouds. Look far
  and wide, across the landscape. Notice trees, buildings,
  architectural and natural details. Take the wide and
  expansive view, and let yourself be amazed by what
  you witness.

Micro-gazing: Look near and close.
* With natural or man-made properties, even if it is
  simply a pencil at your desk. Spend a few moments
  looking at the intricate details of this object. For added
  emphasis, use a magnifying glass to drop into the
  details. Notice how, as you gaze, more details become
  evident. Marvel at such an object in your hands.

The world around you
is quite amazing, if you'll
take just a moment or
two to notice it. Think
of the creativity and/or
industry that
has contributed
to what you see.
Isn't it a wonder?

Inner Wise-Woman

There is a group of "older" women in my community – a "wise-woman" group – who celebrate their ageing as having reached a full expression of experience and wisdom. In fact, a wise-woman is the archetypal figure of someone who is knowledgeable about traditional lore.

Imagine if you could consult your future self, for advice and counsel. What might he or she share with you about inner peace, from their vantage point?

When my daughter was graduating from university, she was stressed with the uncertainty of not knowing her future: where she would live, where she would work, whom she would marry. I suggested that she consult her inner wise-woman, by having her 98-year-old self write a letter to her current self about what she had learned in life. My daughter thought this sounded strange, but she was willing to give it a try. Happily, her older self had some good advice.

Perhaps your own 98-year-old self, even now, has some wisdom to impart to you. Perspective creates the space for inner peace to arise.

- Close your eyes and imagine yourself at the age of 98 years. See if you can create a "visual" of what your future self might look like.
- Formulate a question or a concern that you would like to ask your inner wise-woman.
- Imagine your 98-year-old self conversing with your current self.
- Know that as you imagine this conversation, you are accessing an older, wiser and fully-awake part of yourself, who is familiar with the arc of your life.
- See if a wider perspective shifts your current perception of what is going on today.

Four Directions

In our busy lives it's easy to become so self-involved that we forget about the larger, amazing world of which we are a part.

This simple stretch, paired with focused contemplation, is designed to get you out of yourself and to remind you that you are part of a much bigger world. Imagine yourself as something of a compass, as you salute points east and west, sky and earth, and all the life in those directions. Remember to breathe during this process.

- **Reach your hands high up to the sky.** Start to think about everything that is above you: treetops, birds' nests, flying geese, gliders and aeroplanes, clouds and stars. Imagine all of life that exists above you, including everything beyond this planet and even beyond this galaxy.

- **Reach your hands to the right, bending your body toward the east** (either reaching both hands together or just your outer hand, while your inner hand supports your body at your waist). Think about what lies to the east of you. Imagine an expanse of water to the east, land masses, countries, people you know in those countries, people you don't know in those countries, wild and domesticated animals in those countries, flora and fauna. Think of the sun rising each morning in the east.

- **Reach your hands to the left, bending your body toward the west** (either reaching both hands together or just your outer hand, while your inner hand supports your body at the waist.) Think about what lies to the west of you. Imagine an expanse of water to the west, land masses, countries, people you know in those countries, people you don't know in those countries, wild and domesticated animals in those countries, flora and fauna. Think of the sun setting each evening in the west.

- **Reach your hands to the earth.** Slowly bring your body down into a forward "fold". You can either grab your elbows in a "rag doll" bend or sink, to let your fingers touch your toes. Bend your knees, if that is more comfortable. Breathe. Imagine all of life that is on the surface of our earth . . . ants and other insects, animals, grass and stones. And think too of all the life that exists below "sea level" – the vast worlds of underwater sea life. Think of the plants and fish that live down under.
- **Bring yourself back to a standing pose** and notice how it feels, both to stretch your body and to place yourself in this vast circle of life that exists all around you, of which you are a part.

A Peace Garden

Peace is a journey of a thousand miles
and it must be taken one step at a time.
— *Lyndon B. Johnson*

I hope that this little book and the practices
contained here have helped you access your own
deep peace. I wish for you that the daily use of
these tools and techniques will help you know
that you are not alone, and that you hold the key
to feeling whole.

As you bring peace into your life through these mindful
pauses, the effects will ripple far beyond yourself, in the
following ways:

• becoming grounded and rooted
• relaxing
• practising equanimity
• cultivating acceptance, gratitude and compassion
• looking beyond yourself.

I invite you to join me in cultivating a vast and glorious garden. The seeds already reside within you. Think of each peace practice as a small dose of fertilizer, sunshine and water. As you tend and nurture the garden, the many seeds will sprout. By choosing to engage in these simple but powerful practices, day after day, you will create the conditions for the growth of shoots and roots. Before you know it, flowers will blossom.

Peace flourishes within you.
Peace spreads beyond you.

References

Adyashanti, *Falling into Grace: Insights on the End of Suffering* (Colorado: Sounds True, 2013)

Baraz, J. and Alexander, S., *Awakening Joy: 10 Steps That Will Put You on the Road to Real Happiness* (New York: Bantam, 2010)

Boroson, M., *One-Moment Meditation: Stillness for People on the Go* (New York: Winter Road, 2009)

Bush, A.D., *Shortcuts to Inner Peace: 70 Simple Paths to Everyday Serenity* (New York: Berkley Books, 2011)

Chodron, Pema, *Taking the Leap: Freeing Ourselves from Old Habits and Fears* (Boston: Shambhala, 2010)

Gach, M.R. and Henning, B.A., *Acupressure for Emotional Healing: A Self-Care Guide for Trauma, Stress & Common Emotional Imbalances* (New York: Bantam Dell, 2004)

Germer, C.K., *The Mindful Path to Self-Compassion: Freeing Yourself from Destructive Thoughts and Emotions* (New York: Guilford Press, 2009)

Hanson, R., *Hardwiring Happiness: The New Brain Science of Contentment, Calm, and Confidence* (New York: Harmony, 2013)

Katie, B. and Mitchell, S., *Loving What Is: Four Questions That Can Change Your Life* (New York: Three Rivers Press, 2003)

Ortner, N., *The Tapping Solution: A Revolutionary System for Stress-Free Living* (Carlsbad, CA: Hay House, 2014)

Salzberg, S., *Lovingkindness: The Revolutionary Art of Happiness* (Boston: Shambhala, 2002)

Tolle, E., *The Power of Now: A Guide to Spiritual Enlightenment* (Novato, CA: New World Library, 1999)

Acknowledgements

I am delighted to thank my editor, Leanne Bryan. Leanne was the wise midwife who helped ensure the healthy birth of this book into the world. I am also grateful to Juliette Norsworthy, the inspired art director; to Polly Poulter, the efficient project manager; as well as to the entire amazing team at Octopus Publishing Group. Another grateful nod goes to my loyal literary agent, John Willig, who continues to be a trusted advisor, friend and guide.

To the brothers of the Episcopalian order of St John the Evangelist – thank you for offering me your presence, your hospitality, your teachings and your Spirit for over a decade. To my dearest friend, Martha, may I just say "Om shanti" and thank you for your peaceful presence in my life. And to my amazing husband, Daniel, I offer my open heart and my deeply rooted gratitude for your editing skills, your abundant love and our incredible life together.